DAVID LIVINGSTONE

Please visit our web site at: www.worldalmanaclibrary.com
For a free color catalog describing World Almanac® Library's list of high-quality books
and multimedia programs, call 1-800-848-2928 (USA) or 1-800-387-3178 (Canada).
World Almanac® Library's fax: (414) 332-3567.

Library of Congress Cataloging-in-Publication Data

Freedman, Frances.
    David Livingstone / by Frances Freedman. — North American ed.
       p. cm. — (Great explorers)
    Includes bibliographical references and index.
    Summary: A biography of the Scottish doctor and missionary who is also known
for his explorations in Africa in the nineteenth century.
    ISBN 0-8368-5015-7 (lib. bdg.)
    ISBN 0-8368-5175-7 (softcover)
    1. Livingstone, David, 1813-1873—Juvenile literature.   2. Explorers—Africa, Southern—
Biography—Juvenile literature.   3. Explorers—Scotland—Biography—Juvenile literature.
4. Missionaries, Medical—Africa, Southern—Biography—Juvenile literature.   5. Missionaries,
Medical—Scotland—Biography—Juvenile literature.   [1. Livingstone, David, 1813-1873.
2. Explorers.   3. Missionaries.] I. Title. II. Great explorers (Milwaukee, Wis.)
DT1110.L58F74   2001
916.704'23'092—dc21
[B]   2001026837

This North American edition first published in 2002 by
World Almanac® Library
330 West Olive Street, Suite 100
Milwaukee, Wisconsin 53212 USA

This U.S. edition © 2002 by World Almanac® Library.
Created with original © 2001 by Quartz Editions,
112 Station Road, Edgware HA8 7AQ, U.K.
Additional end matter © 2002 by World Almanac® Library.

Series Editor: Tamara Green
World Almanac® Library editor and contributing writer: Gini Holland
World Almanac® Library project editor: Betsy Rasmussen
World Almanac® Library designer: Melissa Valuch

The creators and publishers of this volume wish to thank the following for their kind permission to feature
illustration material: Front cover: main image, Helen Jones/ other images, Royal Geographical Society/ Pitt-Rivers
Museum, Oxford/ Science & Society, Picture Library/ Bridgeman Art Library/ Stuart Brendon/ Oxford Scientific
Films; Back cover: Royal Geographical Society/ David Livingstone Museum/Bridgeman Art Library; 5 t
Bridgeman Art Library, Royal Geographical Society/ c, b Royal Geographical Society; 6 t Science & Society
Picture Library/ c, b David Livingstone Centre; 7 Helen Jones; 8 t Bridgeman Art Library/ c, b Royal
Geographical Society; 10 Bridgeman Art Library, Royal Geographical Society/ 11 t, c Bridgeman Art Library,
Royal Geographical Society/ b David Livingstone Centre; 12–13 Stuart Brendon; 14 t AKG/ c Bridgeman Art
Library, Wilberforce House, Hull City Museums & Art Galleries/ b The Art Archive; 15 t AKG/ b Bridgeman Art
Library; 16 t Royal Geographical Society/ c, b AKG; 17 t AKG/ b Bridgeman Art Library; 18 t, c Royal
Geographical Society/ b Bridgeman Art Library, Royal Geographical Society; 19 t Bridgeman Art Library, Royal
Geographical Society/ b AKG; 20 Royal Geographical Society; 21 t Bridgeman Art Library/ b Pitt-Rivers Museum;
22 t, c David Livingstone Centre/ b Bridgeman Art Library, Royal Geographical Society; 23 David Livingstone
Centre; 24 t, c Bridgeman Art Library/ b The Art Archive; 25 t The Art Archive/ c, b Royal Geographical Society;
26 t Bridgeman Art Library, Royal Geographical Society/ b AKG; 27 t Bridgeman Art Library, Africana Museum,
Johannesburg/ c The Art Archive/ b Bridgeman Art Library, Royal Geographical Society; 28 t The Art Archive/ c
Natural History Photographic Agency/ b Royal Geographical Society; 30 t Bridgeman Art Library/ b AKG; 31 t
Natural History Photographic Agency/ b Oxford Scientific Films; 32 t Royal Geographical Society/ c AKG/ b
Ancient Art & Architecture Collection; 33 t Natural History Photographic Agency/ b AKG; 34 t Royal
Geographical Society/ c The Art Archive/ b Tony Stone Images; 35 t, 36 t Royal Geographical Society/ 36 c
Bridgeman Art Library, Royal Geographical Society/ b Royal Geographical Society; 38 t David Livingstone Centre/
b AKG; 39 t David Livingstone Centre/ b Bridgeman Art Library, Royal Geographical Society; 40 t David
Livingstone Centre/b AKG; 41 t David Livingstone Centre/ b Bridgeman Art Library, Royal Geographical Society;
42 t Bridgeman Art Library, Natural History Museum, London/ b Bridgeman Art Library; 43 Helen Jones

All rights reserved. No part of this book may be reproduced, stored in a retrieval system, or transmitted in any
form or by any means, electronic, mechanical, photocopying, recording, or otherwise, without the prior written
permission of the copyright holder.

Printed in the United States of America

1 2 3 4 5 6 7 8 9 06 05 04 03 02

DAVID
LIVINGSTONE

FRANCES FREEDMAN

WORLD ALMANAC® LIBRARY

Young Adult Resources $36.60 10/05

CONTENTS

INTRODUCTION

DAVID LIVINGSTONE wanted to explore territory in Africa where no European had ever set foot. This 19th-century Scotsman also had a passion for spreading Christianity and ending the slave trade.

Livingstone succeeded in navigating some of Africa's many rivers (*above*).

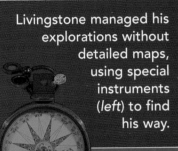

Livingstone managed his explorations without detailed maps, using special instruments (*left*) to find his way.

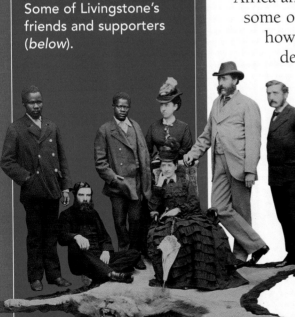

Some of Livingstone's friends and supporters (*below*).

David Livingstone was a man of many interests. He had some formal medical training. He was also familiar with astronomy, paleontology, botany, mathematics, anthropology, Latin, and ancient Greek. In many of these subjects he was self-taught.

He might well have gone on to have an outstanding academic career, but he was an intensely religious man, and he decided to become a Christian missionary. His intent was to spread the word of God. In 1840, he set out on his first voyage to Africa and spent the next 33 years exploring there.

Livingstone explored the lands and waterways of Africa and may well have been the first European to see some of that continent's most beautiful sights. It was, however, his respect for the African people and his desire to see an end to the slave trade that drove him to continue his explorations through severe hardships. His close contact with, and reliance on, various African people allowed him to learn about and appreciate cultures and traditions different from his own.

Although he failed in his original intent to convert Africans to Christianity, he succeeded as a humanitarian by doing his part to educate the people of Europe about the evils of slavery.

DAVID LIVINGSTONE

MAN OF FAITH

Livingstone's training as a medical practitioner was an advantage throughout his travels. This is his portable medicine chest (*left*).

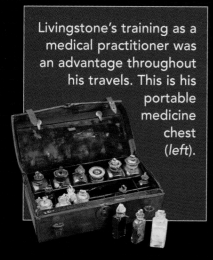

A gold medal (*right*) was awarded to Livingstone in 1855 by the Royal Geographical Society, London.

Livingstone always kept meticulous illustrated notes, like those in his field notebook (*below*), and he kept a daily diary.

Honors were heaped on Livingstone, yet he always remained a modest and hardworking man as he struggled to open up Africa to commerce and Christianity.

David Livingstone was born on March 19, 1813, and raised in poverty in the mill town of Blantyre, just outside Glasgow, Scotland. His parents, Neil and Agnes Livingstone, had seven children, five of whom — three boys and two girls — survived infancy. His father made a meager living as a traveling tea salesman.

All the family members had to live and sleep in a single room in a run-down tenement building. David was schooled at home until he turned ten; then he was sent to work as a "piecer" at the mill. Six days a week, from six o'clock in the morning until eight at night, he scrambled among the spinning machines, piecing together broken strands of cotton thread. After this 14-hour workday, each child received two hours of schooling. Despite the hardships of work, David retained a love of learning. He used part of his first week's pay to buy a Latin textbook. He stayed up late at night, studying Latin, mathematics, and science. He also enjoyed travel books.

David's father was not enthusiastic about David's interest in science. Neil Livingstone believed that science would weaken his son's religious beliefs.

> *I am a missionary, heart and soul. . . . In this service, I hope to live. In it, I wish to die.*

MEDICAL MISSIONARY

At the age of 19, David Livingstone bought a book by Dr. Thomas Dick, a minister who was also an amateur astronomer. This book changed David's life. It persuaded him that he could study the natural sciences and still be a good Christian.

At about this time, David learned that there was a need for missionaries who had medical training. Choosing to be a doctor as well as a missionary would allow him to pursue his interest in science and religion. It would also allow him to minister to people's bodies in addition to their souls.

In 1836, he enrolled at the medical school of the Andersonian University in Glasgow. Two years later, he was accepted for training by the London Missionary Society. His missionary training included studies in Latin, Greek, and Hebrew — all of limited practical use when attempting to speak with the people of Africa.

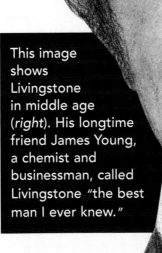

This image shows Livingstone in middle age (*right*). His longtime friend James Young, a chemist and businessman, called Livingstone "the best man I ever knew."

This oil painting (*left*) by Horatio McCulloch shows a street in 19th-century Glasgow, Scotland, not far from where David Livingstone spent his childhood.

ETERNAL OPTIMIST

A great friend, William Cotton Oswell, described Livingstone as being "patient, all-enduring under hardships, content to win his way by inches, but never swerving from it." Not even when he was so weak that he had to be carried on his travels did he give up. He was, in many respects, the eternal optimist.

Livingstone also believed it was important to have, as he put it, "constant employment and sufficient bodily exercise to produce perspiration every day." Indeed, he constantly drove himself to his physical limits.

This cap (*right*) is the very one that Livingstone famously raised when found by Henry Morton Stanley at Ujiji (in what is now Tanzania) on November 10, 1871. The meeting prompted Stanley to give the well-known greeting: "Dr. Livingstone, I presume." The hat now belongs to the Royal Geographical Society of London.

This section of a stump (*right*) was taken from a tree in a village in central Africa, underneath which David Livingstone's heart was buried in a tin box. This portion of the tree is now held in the collection of the Royal Geographical Society.

NATURE LOVER

Livingstone was a lover of natural history. As a boy, he had been interested in plants, animals, and fossils. While exploring Africa, he filled many notebooks with details about the countless varieties of plants and animals he observed there.

He described, for instance, the way a certain bird, a species of plover, would help crocodiles clean their teeth by pecking inside their open jaws. The crocodiles did not seem to mind this and simply let the birds go ahead with their work.

Not surprisingly, he also hated killing animals. As he put it to his team, "I would earnestly impress on every member of the Expedition a sacred regard to life, and never to destroy it unless some good end is to be answered by its extinction." He was also appalled by the ivory trade, which involved the slaughter of elephants; and yet, he did agree to the killing of some forms of wildlife during the course of his expeditions because he needed a source of food with which to feed his men.

Livingstone also opposed the cruel treatment of human beings. He spent much of his life working to abolish the brutal slave trade that he witnessed in Africa.

Livingstone first wanted to go to China as a missionary, but war in China made that impossible. After meeting Robert Moffat, also a missionary, he decided, "I will at once go to Africa." In 1845, he married Moffat's daughter, Mary, who had been raised in Africa.

> *Nothing will make me give up my work in despair. I encourage myself in the Lord and go forward.*

DETERMINED TRAVELER

Livingstone spent more than 30 years in Africa, seeking converts to Christianity and trade for Great Britain.

During his first journeys, between 1841 and 1853, he explored southern Africa, all the way from the southern tip of the continent to the region the British called Barotseland, now the independent nation of Zambia. During the next three years (1853–56), he explored the Zambezi River — a journey that eventually took him all the way from the eastern shores of Mozambique to the west coast of Angola. This journey, during which he arrived at, and named, Victoria Falls, made him a hero in Britain.

Livingstone continued to explore the Zambezi region between 1858 and 1864. He spent his remaining years in what turned out to be an unsuccessful quest for the source of the world's longest river, the mighty Nile.

DIFFERENT VIEWPOINTS

Livingstone was highly praised by most people who knew him. Some people, however, found him lacking certain qualities.

He did not excel as a preacher, and the London Missionary Society's principal even described him as coarse and with a heaviness of manner. Some thought he was obsessive because, when pursuing a dangerous course, he risked not only his own life, but also his wife's. In 1862, she died of malaria on the banks of the Zambezi.

Despite great difficulties, Livingstone kept his faith. He was always sure that, with God's help, all would be right in the end.

1813
David Livingstone is born in Scotland.

1840
Livingstone is ordained as a Christian missionary.

1841
Livingstone arrives in Africa for the first time.

1844
Livingstone sets up a mission at Mabotsa.

1845
Livingstone marries.

1849
Livingstone reaches Lake Ngami.

1855
Livingstone arrives at, and names, Victoria Falls.

1856
Livingstone completes journey from east coast to west coast of Africa.

1858-64
Livingstone explores the Zambezi River.

1866
Livingstone begins search for source of the Nile River.

1871
Livingstone meets Stanley.

1873
Livingstone dies in Africa.

THE CHALLENGE OF AFRICA

This painting by Thomas Baines (*above*), who was with Livingstone in Africa, shows wagons making their way through Cape Province, South Africa.

The paddle steamer *Ma Robert*, which was used by Livingstone, is shown in a painting by Baines (*below*). The noises it made seemed to frighten the elephants.

Sometimes it was easier for Livingstone's party to travel on foot than by wagon, as depicted in a picture by Baines (*right*).

Europeans saw Africa as a source of raw materials and cheap labor and as a market for European products. But penetrating Africa's heartland was no easy matter.

Like most Europeans of his day, David Livingstone regarded Europe as more "civilized" than Africa. As a missionary, he thought that Christian Europeans had a responsibility to share their beliefs with less "civilized" peoples.

Other Europeans came to Africa for very different reasons. They wanted to take African resources — ivory, gold, diamonds, and rubber. They wanted to employ Africans at wages much lower than Europeans would accept. They also thought they could persuade Africans to buy products made in Europe. This would mean more jobs for European factory workers and bigger profits for the European factory owners.

During the 19th century, Britain, France, and Germany all scrambled to create imperial governments in Africa. Imperialism is the term that describes an effort by one country to dominate the economic, political, and cultural life of another.

Before Europeans could take control of Africa, they had to penetrate from the seacoasts into the interior. Sometimes Livingstone's crew had to use axes to hack a path through grasses that towered at least 2 feet (.6 meter) above their heads. At other times, the expedition trudged for days over vast areas of scrubland with the missionary on the back of his ox, Sinbad.

Once, when Livingstone was ill with a high fever, he insisted on continuing to ride through boggy land in a heavy rainstorm. Sinbad bolted, throwing Livingstone. Later, he said, "I felt none the worse for this rough treatment, but would not recommend it to others as a palliative in cases of fever."

In 1867, as he made further inroads into Africa, Livingstone is known to have remarked, "The country is a succession of enormous waves, all covered with jungle, and no traces of paths." Every now and then, however, the explorer came across views that charmed him. On reaching a small lake, for example, he said, "The sight of the blue waters, and the waves lashing the shore, had a most soothing influence on the mind after so much lifeless, flat, and gloomy forest."

MAKING HEADWAY

SENSE OF DIRECTION
The Royal Geographical Society in London has in its collection the compass (*above*) used on the first of David Livingstone's journeys. Without such an instrument, it would have been practically impossible to maintain any sense of direction when traveling to the heart of Africa during the 19th century. This was prior to the railway age, and the only means of wheeled transportation widely available was covered wagons (*below*). Livingstone traveled by wagon from the south coast of Africa to Kuruman, a journey of about 700 miles (1,126 kilometers). It would have been a very bumpy ride over rugged terrain. Sometimes Livingstone chose to go on foot, and other times he rode on

ox-back. This, too, was an uncomfortable mode of travel. Often the ox would use its horns to give its rider a nasty blow in the side or stomach. To avoid that, Livingstone was obliged to sit as upright as possible for long periods of time.

ABOARD THE *MA ROBERT*
Another method of transportation used by Livingstone when traveling along the Zambezi River was a paddle steamer named the *Ma Robert* (*below*). Livingstone had the vessel built in England for reassembly in Africa. Originally constructed in record time (just five weeks), it was 75 feet

(23 m) long and had a 12-horse-power engine. There was room for up to 36 passengers, and the vessel could hold sufficient cargo for a two-year African expedition. Two years was the length of time Livingstone initially anticipated for the journey. Instead, he spent from 1858 to 1864 on this Zambezi expedition. The paddle steamer, called by the same name the Africans gave Livingstone's wife, fell to pieces toward the end of 1860, however.

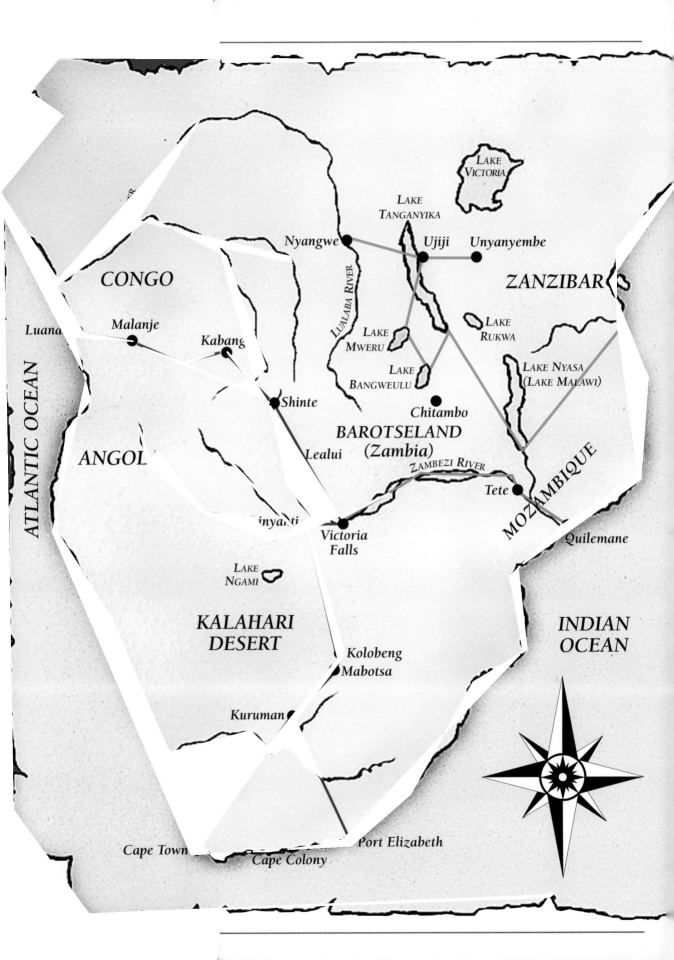

LIVINGSTONE'S
AFRICAN JOURNEYS

AT VICTORIA FALLS

"It was the most wonderful sight I had witnessed in Africa." These were the words that Livingstone used to describe the Falls after seeing them for the first time in November 1855. Awestruck by their beauty, he named them after England's Queen Victoria.

A FAMOUS ENCOUNTER

On November 10, 1871, at Ujiji, on the shore of Lake Tanganyika, the American reporter and adventurer Henry Morton Stanley finally found the great Scottish explorer and met him with a greeting that would become legendary: "Dr. Livingstone, I presume."

INTO THE HEART OF AFRICA

It was Livingstone's desire to spread the word of Christianity that first led him to make his African expeditions. Not unexpectedly, making progress through uncharted territory was riddled with problems. Lack of suitable transportation was just one of those challenges. Livingstone relied on an ox-driven wagon for the 700-mile (1,126-km) journey from Cape Town to Kuruman. After that, he traveled mostly on foot, hacking paths through thick jungle. While exploring the Zambezi River, he used his paddle steamer, the *Ma Robert*, for the length of time that the river remained navigable.

In his travels, Livingstone faced such obstacles as malarial swamps and a near-fatal attack by a lion at Mabotsa. He often found it difficult to work with his fellow Europeans, and people who made their living from slave trading regarded him with hostility or suspicion. Livingstone's journeys covered huge distances. His achievements are all the more remarkable in view of the tremendous challenges he surmounted.

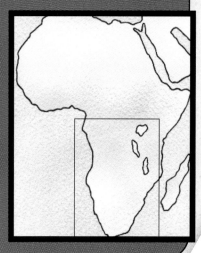

KEY

———	EXPEDITIONS 1841-1856
———	TRAVELS 1858-1864
———	LAST EXPEDITION 1866-1873

FIGHTING THE SLAVE TRADE

Purchasers of slaves always chose the strongest of the group (*above*).

Am I Not a Man and a Brother? is the title of this anonymous painting (*below*).

The slaves in this detail from a watercolor (*right*) are typical of those in the many chain gangs Livingstone set out to release.

From the moment he first saw a man in chains, David Livingstone resolved to do all he could to free the captives and put a stop to the slave trade in Africa.

One of Livingstone's main purposes in "opening up" Africa was to encourage commerce. Unlike some other Europeans, however, his support for trade did not stem from greed or self-interest. Instead, he hoped that commerce in raw materials and manufactured goods would lead people to stop trading in slaves.

As Livingstone said in 1857, in Edinburgh, Scotland, "I hope to be able to make a path by the Zambezi into the central country; and then, if we can supply the people with our goods for lawful commerce, I think we have a fair prospect of putting a stop to the slave trade in a very large tract of country."

Livingstone wanted to get the people of central Africa to trade with one another so that they would begin to develop a mutual dependence. He also wanted to encourage them to start manufacturing for the English.

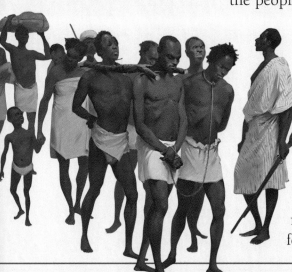

> ***If we enter in and form a settlement, we shall be able in the course of a very few years to put a stop to the slave trade in that quarter.*** **"**

SPREADING THE NEWS

"Commerce," Livingstone said, "is a most important aid in diffusing the blessings of Christianity because one tribe never goes to another without telling the news, and the Gospel comes to be part of the news."

Livingstone also expressed the view that if Great Britain started to get supplies of raw materials, such as cotton, from the African continent instead of from the United States, slaveholders in North America might at last become more enlightened and eventually realize that they did not need to own slaves.

The buying and selling of people was loathsome to Livingstone. The Act of Abolition, passed in 1833, had for the most part stopped such trading on the west coast of Africa, but the slave trade openly persisted in Africa's central and eastern regions. Wherever he traveled, Livingstone found plundered villages, ruined crops, and rotting corpses abandoned by slave traders.

When he arrived at Lake Nyasa on September 16, 1859, Livingstone discovered that Lake Nyasa — a large body of water in Eastern Africa, now often called Lake Malawi — was situated on one of the main slave routes leading to the coast. As his party rested at a village, they were approached by slavers who offered to sell them children. They refused, of course, but Livingstone later wondered if they should perhaps have purchased the boys so that they would not be sold elsewhere.

Livingstone then wrote to his home government, urging the creation of a British colony in the Lake Nyasa region. If the British took over the area, he thought, the slave trade could be stopped. At that time, however, Britain did not want any more colonies, and Livingstone's proposal was rejected. Not until the end of the 19th century did the British take control of Nyasaland (now the independent nation of Malawi).

CARGO

When we think of a ship's cargo, we usually think of cartons of goods for trade, along with supplies to sustain the crew during a lengthy voyage. When the slave trade was in full force, however, some ships were specially fitted out so they could carry as much human cargo as possible (*right*). Conditions on board the ship were terrible, and many of the slaves perished before reaching their destination. Some starved to death; others died from contagious diseases or because of the lack of sanitation. In this print (*below*), a group of Africans show fear for their future as they are about to be taken out of a captured dhow, a type of Arab ship.

Arab slave hunters launch an attack on an African village (*above*). Livingstone estimated that only about one in ten of such slaves would survive to be sold after capture.

slaves. On one occasion, he came upon a market where former inhabitants of a Congo forest, now to be traded as slaves, had been gathered to walk eastward to the coast. For some reason, on this very hot July day in 1871, tempers flared and guns were fired. Some slaves were shot. Others, seeking safety, jumped in a nearby river and drowned. At least 400 Africans died that day.

Livingstone devoted much of his time in Africa to his effort to stamp out the slave trade. In the course of his activities, he sometimes made enemies of slave traders. At times, however, he had little choice but to accept their help. It was slave traders from Zanzibar — the very slave traders Livingstone was trying to put out of business — who at one point rescued and nursed him when, malnourished, he fell seriously ill with rheumatic fever and dysentery.

SENSELESS CRUELTY
Livingstone observed many tragic incidents involving

Livingstone also began to feel intense resentment toward Portugal as a nation. The Portuguese government had maintained a presence in the Zambezi Valley for over 300 years. Britain was prepared not to dispute the Portuguese claim to this land, as long as Portugal agreed not to interfere with British antislavery activities. Not anxious to antagonize the British, the Portuguese government agreed to support Livingstone's humanitarian efforts, even helping to equip an anti-slavery expedition. Livingstone, however, soon realized that the Portuguese were not adequately controlling the slave trade. He could see people under Portuguese rule still buying and selling lives.

He even believed his own explorations might have contributed to the spread of the slave trade. Earlier, the Portuguese — who occupied what today are the independent nations of Angola and Mozambique — would not have traveled into some parts of Africa. Now, slave traders seemed to be following behind him — some even falsely claiming to be part of his expedition.

MEMBERS OF THE TEAM

Some slaves were lucky enough to gain their freedom. One of them, Chuma, had been released while still a nine-year-old boy. He was found by Livingstone in India and joined his team. Another former slave, Susi, was also befriended by Livingstone.

Both men accompanied the missionary on all his later travels. Indeed, he became increasingly dependent on

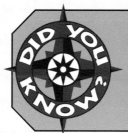

Some African chiefs, Livingstone reported, were willing to sell their own family members to slave traders in exchange for fabric. According to Livingstone, the going rate for a male slave was just 4 yards (3.66 m) of cloth; for a female slave, 3 yards (2.74 m); and for a child, 2 yards (1.83 m).

them during his last years. They even carried his body to Zanzibar after his death. In 1874, they were brought to England, where they helped get Livingstone's final journal ready for publication.

66 *Dead bodies floated past daily, and in the mornings, paddles had to be cleared of corpses caught in the night.* 99

This image (*above*) shows a group of adults and children in a typical Ethiopian slave caravan in about the year 1842. In this part of Africa, the slave market was just as active as it was in those regions of the continent explored by Livingstone.

Livingstone's efforts to end slavery in Africa contributed to the destruction of slave dhows in Zanzibar (*right*) after his death.

This African (*above*) had his portrait painted by Livingstone's fellow-traveler Thomas Baines in 1859.

Livingstone met Africans of various religions. This man (*left*) is wearing verses from the Koran, the Muslim sacred text, in a necklace.

Thomas Baines painted this scene (*right*) while with Livingstone at Tete, where some of the Makololo people settled for a while.

MEETING NATIVE CULTURES

During his time in Africa, Livingstone met many different native cultures and learned a lot about their customs. He had certain favorite cultures, including those of Angola and Makololo.

The African people who Livingstone said he liked most of all were the Makololo. Their chief was Sebetuane, who was succeeded on his death by Sekelutu, only 18 at the time. Livingstone described the Makololo as "very confiding and affectionate," but their dances seemed bizarre to his 19th-century European eyes.

STRANGE STEPS

Writing about such dances, Livingstone recalled that they involved "the men standing nearly naked in a circle, with clubs or small axes in their hands, and each roaring at the loudest pitch of his voice, while they simultaneously lift one leg, stamp heavily twice with it, then lift the other and give one stamp with it. . . . The arms and head are thrown about also in every direction."

Some cultures dressed and decorated their bodies in interesting ways, too. The Batoka (or Batonga), for example, would chip away at their two front incisor teeth, but Livingstone could not find out why. They also wore their hair in a highly ornamental way, piling it

> **We soon learned to forget color, and we frequently saw countenances resembling those of . . . people we had known in England.**

EXCEPTIONAL TALENT

The Batoka were also bold hunters, expert canoers, and skilled musicians. They played an instrument known as a sansa. This instrument, sometimes called a hand piano, consists of thin strips of wood or iron attached to a board, pressed by the fingers, and then released to create a vibrating sound. Another instrument used by the Batoka was the marimba. The marimba is similar to the sansa but is struck with sticks, like a xylophone.

on top of their heads. They would then grease this high column of hair to keep it rigid. The final touch was a spike or bamboo comb.

In addition, Livingstone had to learn the etiquette of various cultural groups so that he did not risk offending them. He learned, for example, that when accepting a gift from a man of the Batoka people, you should expect him to slap his thigh with one hand and that you should do the same when offering something in return. The Batoka manner of greeting was also unusual by European standards. They would throw themselves onto their backs, roll from side to side, and then slap the outside of their thighs while shouting.

Livingstone described the Manganja people, who lived in the Shire Valley (now part of Malawi), as very industrious in the production of cotton. He also considered the Manganja highly advanced in the field of women's rights, because the women of that culture could rise to become chiefs.

Livingstone found one custom of the Manganja's strange. They wore an ornament called a pelele to make the upper lip protrude.

Clothing like this (*above*) was worn by some Africans in the 19th century.

This engraving (*right*) depicts one of the many displays of African dancing that Livingstone came across in the region of the Zambezi River.

Livingstone's coffin (*left*) lying in the map room at the Royal Geographical Society in Savile Row, London, in April 1874, before being conveyed to the funeral at Westminster Abbey. Burial in the Abbey was and still is a great honor.

Livingstone must have been greatly disappointed that he did not make many converts during his time in Africa. Spreading Christianity had, after all, been his principal goal.

The African people would listen attentively to what he had to say and watched with interest and curiosity when he showed them lantern slides illustrating Bible stories. He was unable to persuade them to put the lessons he preached into practice, however.

When Livingstone returned to England in 1856, he was greeted by the public as a hero. The London Missionary Society, however, was less than thrilled. His travels were expensive and dangerous and were attracting more publicity in England than converts in Africa.

The society wanted Livingstone to become a settled missionary, remaining in one place instead of traveling across the continent. This Livingstone refused to do. The Society withdrew its financial backing, and Livingstone resigned his membership. With support from the British government, he was able to continue his efforts to stop the slave trade and bring commerce to Africa. He believed evangelism would follow after he had succeeded on these fronts.

All the while his faith remained constant. He read the Bible every day and prayed regularly and fervently for the strength, both mental and physical, to continue his work. "The sweat of one's brow is no longer a curse when one works for God; it proves a tonic to the system, and is actually a blessing," he wrote. When desperate, he would beg for God's intervention. "Leave me not, forsake me not. I cast myself and all my cares down at thy feet. Thou knowest all I need, for time and for eternity."

Exploring the uncharted regions of Africa was a dangerous and sometimes lonely task. He would surely have found it difficult to continue his explorations had he not been sustained by his deep religious beliefs. "I need to be purified, fitted for the eternal, to which my soul stretches in ever-returning longings," Livingstone wrote in a journal entry for February 19, 1854. "I need to be made more like my blessed Saviour, to serve my God with all my powers." He concluded his prayer with this impassioned plea: "Look upon me, Spirit of the living God, and supply all Thou seest lacking."

The Makololo were amazed when they saw the sea for the first time. They had always believed that the world comprised just one extensive plain. After trekking with Livingstone to the coast, they now saw that there was an end to the stretch of land they had crossed.

The pelele, which the Manganja thought to be a sign of beauty, could be made from tin, clay, or quartz. The Manganja also tattooed their faces and bodies.

The Manganja enjoyed drinking an alcoholic substance made from grain. The grain was pounded, mixed with water, boiled, and allowed to thicken and ferment. Livingstone noted that the pink beverage was strong but thirst quenching.

Livingstone saw in this culture much that he admired in his own culture and said, "We soon learned to forget color, and we frequently saw countenances resembling those of . . . people we had known in England."

SPIRITUAL BELIEFS

Livingstone described many interesting spiritual beliefs among the people he encountered. The dead were said to remain in contact with their relatives and sometimes appeared in unusual forms.

Once, for instance, when a man was about to sell his canoe, he suddenly spotted a large snake on the branch of a nearby tree. He immediately canceled the deal, convinced that the reptile was in fact his father's spirit returning to object to the sale.

Innocence of a crime, it was also believed, could be proven simply by taking a poisonous drink. If the individual survived, the verdict was innocent; if death occurred, the verdict was guilty.

SUPPORTERS AND FRIENDS

Livingstone's wife, Mary (*above*), stuck by him in spite of his absences. She often had to care for their children on her own.

Wealthy William Cotton Oswell (*below*) provided welcomed funding for Livingstone's expeditions. They met for the first time when Oswell was in Africa on safari, hunting elephants for ivory.

Livingstone named the Murchison Falls after Roderick Murchison (*right*), who was instrumental in getting aid from the British government for further exploration.

A great many people, both Europeans and Africans, helped Livingstone in the course of his travels. Without them, he could never have achieved as much as he did.

Many of the friendships that Livingstone made survived for his entire life. The first person to assist him in Africa, for instance, was Robert Moffat, the man who later became his father-in-law. Moffat, a noted evangelist and preacher, had been running the missionary station at Kuruman in Bechuanaland (now Botswana) since 1823. It was to this mission that Livingstone was first assigned in 1841 at the age of 28. Moffat was generous with the advice he gave to the newcomer, and the family took Livingstone in when he became ill.

FAITHFUL WIFE

The woman who nursed Livingstone through his illness was Robert Moffat's daughter Mary. She had been educated in Africa and spoke Setswana, an important language of southern Africa. In January 1845, she and Livingstone were married. Together they founded a mission at Chonwane.

In one letter, Livingstone described Mary somewhat unflatteringly as "a little thick black-haired girl, sturdy and all I want." Mary was a selfless and faithful wife, giving birth in the wilderness, raising their children under the most intolerable conditions, and enduring long periods of poor health, terrible weather, and lack of hygiene.

> **❝** *Oh, long as we were parted, ever since you went away, I never passed an easy night, or knew an easy day.* **❞**
> MARY LIVINGSTONE

She and the Livingstones' four surviving children were sent back to Britain in 1852. There she suffered both the sadness of separation from her husband and the sting of poverty. She returned with him to Africa in 1858 but died of malaria in 1862.

FINANCIAL SUPPORT

One of Livingstone's most important friends and backers was a wealthy Englishman, William Cotton Oswell. He and Livingstone first met when Oswell stopped off at the missionary station in Mabotsa, before going on safari.

Oswell gave generously to support one of Livingstone's expeditions, and in 1849, the two men traveled together — along with two other Europeans and 38 Africans — across the Kalahari Desert to Lake Ngami. Oswell also joined Livingstone on a second northern trek in 1851 and contributed a lot more money to Livingstone's later activities.

Much of Oswell's money came from trading the ivory tusks of elephants he had shot. Although Livingstone disapproved of big-game hunting, he was still willing to accept Oswell's backing and friendship. When Mary Livingstone gave birth to a boy in 1851, he was named William Oswell Livingstone in recognition of Oswell's assistance.

Livingstone received other kinds of help, too. Thomas Maclear, the Astronomer Royal, taught Livingstone how to make maps. Maclear was later to observe that Livingstone's maps of the African continent were among the most accurate he had ever seen. "His observations of the course of the Zambezi . . . are the finest specimens of geographical observation I ever met with," he wrote.

Several eminent British organizations benefited Livingstone, too. The Royal Geographical Society offered praise and awarded a gold medal, which must in turn

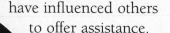

Queen Victoria of Great Britain (*right*) whole-heartedly approved of Livingstone's work in Africa.

Henry Morton Stanley (*above*) was only 30 years old when he found Livingstone and helped nurse him back to health.

This engraving (*right*) shows Livingstone and Stanley reading. They got along well and shared many activities during their short time together.

have influenced others to offer assistance. The Foreign Office in London, for example, provided Livingstone with a grant for the construction of a paddle steamer. Queen Victoria, who approved of what Livingstone was trying to achieve, granted him an audience. The queen is said to have laughed heartily when Livingstone recounted that an African chief had inquired as to how many cows she had. Livingstone explained that in Africa, the number of cattle you owned was a measure of your wealth and power.

Victoria reigned over Britain for most of Livingstone's lifetime. She assumed the throne in 1837, when Livingstone was 24 years old, and outlived the explorer by 28 years.

AFRICAN AID

Not all the Africans Livingstone met were friendly to him. In fact, he once sent a warning to an English acquaintance who was ready to come to Africa as an evangelist: "Don't expect to find the chiefs friendly to missionaries. In general, they are hostile."

Nevertheless, Livingstone did form strong friendships with some African leaders. For a period of six months, he lived among the Bakwena at Chonwane. In this way, he wrote, he gained "an insight into the habits, ways of thinking, laws, and language, which has proved of incalculable advantage."

In particular, Livingstone had high hopes that Chief Sechele of the Bakwena people would embrace Christianity. These hopes were not dampened even when Sechele expressed strong doubts that Livingstone would ever be able to convert an African merely by telling him or her about Christianity.

Sechele himself, meanwhile, seems to have been Livingstone's first true convert. He agreed to be baptized even though it meant sending three of his four wives back to their families and keeping only the first. Livingstone's joy

People often turn to their pets for emotional support, and Livingstone was no exception. Sometimes, when the stresses of the journey threatened to overwhelm them, Livingstone and his crew would be cheered by the frolicking of his pet poodle, Chitane.

at seeing this African leader accept the Christian faith turned sour not long after, when he learned that Sechele had resumed contact with one of the rejected wives and that she was pregnant. "My heart is broken," Livingstone wrote the chief. "I can no longer be a teacher here."

It was Sechele who suggested to Livingstone that he should visit Chief Sebituane of the Makololo people, in Barotseland (now Zambia). The Makololo people's help in hacking paths through the thick rain forests of central Africa

proved extremely valuable.

Precisely why the Makololo offered so much help to Livingstone is unclear. Some historians have pointed to Livingstone's own feeling that some of the people may have believed he had special powers. Whether they actually believed this or not, Livingstone wrote in his journals that on one occasion, when he explained how printed cotton and beads (used as trading items) were manufactured, they responded, "Truly, you are gods!"

Livingstone was so weak near the end of his life that he had to rely on his African friends to help him get around (*above*).

Two days before Livingstone died, this man (*right*) helped him cross a river. The explorer kept going despite his poor health.

Among the group attending Livingstone's funeral (*left*) at London's Westminster Abbey were his two attendants, Susi and Chuma. It was declared a day of national mourning.

A FAMOUS MEETING

Livingstone hated killing of any kind and had an affinity with animals. But there were times during his expeditions when food was in such short supply that he was forced to turn a blind eye to slaughter (*above*).

Livingstone had many narrow escapes, but one of his luckiest moments was definitely when Henry Morton Stanley tracked him down in the heart of Africa.

"Dr. Livingstone, I presume." This is the now world-famous phrase with which newspaper reporter Henry Morton Stanley greeted the explorer David Livingstone. Many assumed Livingstone had been lost in the African heartland or that he was dead. For two years, no one had received a letter from him.

It was the morning of November 10, 1871, when Stanley found Livingstone. By then, he was in poor condition, both physically and mentally. He was living in extreme poverty and was close to starvation. All his worldly goods had been stolen. Never before had the explorer's morale been so low.

Travel in the remote regions of Africa was so difficult that it was pure good luck that brought Henry Morton Stanley to the very spot where Livingstone was living. Their meeting (*right*) did not happen entirely by chance, however. Stanley had been hired to find Livingstone.

Indeed, it was almost with disbelief that he heard his attendant Susi suddenly shout, "An Englishman! I can see him!" as a white man approached at the head of a safari. Livingstone, however, immediately recognized the stars and stripes on the flag advancing toward them and knew Susi was mistaken. The man approaching must be an American!

> **❝I never found a fault in him . . . with Livingstone, each day's life added to my admiration.❞**
>
> H. M. STANLEY

Livingstone could not believe his eyes. "Bales of goods, baths of tin, huge kettles, cooking pots, tents . . . made me think this must be a luxurious traveler, and not one at his wits' end like me," he later wrote.

Everyone present was overjoyed. Against all odds, Stanley had succeeded in finding Livingstone at Ujiji. What was more, he had brought medical supplies, letters from Livingstone's surviving family, and even a bottle of champagne so they could celebrate the occasion in style.

Why had Stanley, a journalist at the time, come all the way from the United States to look for Livingstone?

Most Africans hated the Boer settlers (*above and below*). Between 1899 and 1902, the British fought against the Boers for control of southern Africa.

Crocodiles were a threat to Livingstone and his expedition as they traveled along African rivers. This painting by Thomas Baines (*right*) shows one of the large reptiles being violently subdued.

It was, in fact, the owner of the *New York Herald*, James Gordon Bennett, who had hired the reporter to seek Livingstone out. What Bennett wanted, and got, was an interesting newspaper story. Livingstone, however, was so generous by nature that he considered the publisher's investment of money, time, and energy as a truly splendid gesture. As the explorer modestly put it, "This disinterested kindness of Mr. Bennett, so nobly carried into effect by Mr. Stanley, was simply overwhelming."

This decorated title page (*right*) is from a 19th-century book about Livingstone's many achievements. Historians agree that what he accomplished was certainly against all odds. Historians also view such books as part of an attempt by Europeans of that time to glorify their own efforts to seize control of the African continent.

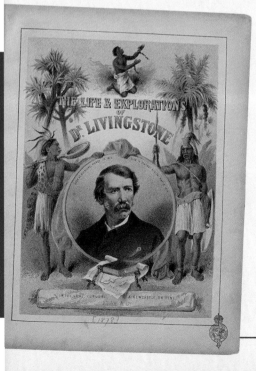

GOOD COMPANIONS

Right from the start, Stanley and Livingstone enjoyed each other's company and seemed to bring out the best in each other. They shared a mutual admiration and had a similar sense of humor. As a result of Stanley's arrival and the supplies he brought with him, Livingstone's health improved and his spirits lifted. Yet, in many ways, the two men were very different.

For a start, there was an enormous age gap — Stanley was younger than Livingstone by almost 30 years. Their backgrounds were also quite different. Livingstone, though of humble origins, had been born into what was considered a traditional two-parent family. Stanley, born in North Wales, had been raised in a Victorian orphanage, where the conditions were horrible. It is perhaps not surprising that Stanley quickly came to regard Livingstone as a father figure.

Just a few days after Stanley's arrival at Ujiji, the two men set off together by canoe to explore part of Lake Tanganyika. One of his main goals, Livingstone explained to Stanley, was to discover whether a certain river flowed out

DID YOU KNOW?

After his famous meeting with Livingstone, Stanley went on to explore the Congo region, supported by King Leopold II of Belgium. Under Leopold's rule, the people and resources of the Congo were ruthlessly exploited — a grim chapter in the history of European imperialism.

of Lake Tanganyika on to Lake Albert and then to the River Nile. Investigation proved, however, that the river only flowed *into* Lake Tanganyika.

Not discouraged by this discovery, the two men now resolved to trek eastward all the way to Unyanyembe, a journey that would take them seven weeks.

> **❝ His gentleness never forsakes him; his hopefulness never deserts him . . . though his heart yearns for home. ❞**
> H. M. STANLEY

Livingstone had hoped to receive a large shipment of supplies at Unyanyembe. He was distraught to find that only a few things remained there for him. A gang of thieves had struck, and he was left with just a few shirts and some boots.

There seemed to be no local people there who were trained to serve as porters for another journey to locate the source of the Nile. Stanley immediately volunteered to go to Zanzibar to find such a team of men. He said goodbye to Livingstone, after having enjoyed about four months in his company. With him, Stanley took along Livingstone's canvas bag, into which were sewn many letters and journals for delivery to England.

Stanley was true to his word and sent porters from Zanzibar who joined Livingstone about five months later. Stanley made the journey to England, where he found that he, too, had become world famous. With backing from England's *Daily Telegraph* newspaper and from Bennett in the United States, he then headed back to Africa, where he pursued his own extraordinary career as an explorer.

HEALTH REPORT

Livingstone was in a poor state of health when Stanley found him. Among other problems, poor nutrition had caused trouble with his teeth. They were rotting, so he resorted to pulling them out.

The method he used seemed brutal, but it worked. He simply tied one end of a string to a rotten tooth, tied the other end of the string to a tree stump, and hit the string with a stick to force the tooth out. Other ailments he had included sores on his feet, repeated fevers, and dysentery.

NEVER SAY DIE

In one of the most frightening events of his many years in Africa, Livingstone was suddenly attacked by a lion (*above*). The beast left him with a wound, and he was never again able to lift his left arm above shoulder level. The lion was shot dead by one of Livingstone's men.

Livingstone rides in an ox-cart near the mission station he set up at Mabotsa (*below*). There he meets some of the local people, who are naturally wary at first.

Already weakened by his journey, Livingstone somehow managed to survive an attack by a lion in Africa. He succeeded in surviving many other hardships, as well.

"Starting, and looking half around, I saw the lion just in the act of springing upon me. . . . Growling horribly close to my ear, he shook me as a terrier dog does a rat."

This is how Livingstone recorded an attack by a lion not long after his arrival in Africa. It was certainly not an ideal start to his work as a missionary. Although surprised by the attack, he did not panic. His instinct was to stay very calm, and this worked to his advantage. What happened next is best described in the missionary's own words: "Turning round to relieve myself of the weight, as he had one paw on the back of my head, I saw his eyes directed to Mebalwe [a porter] who was trying to shoot him at a distance of ten or fifteen yards. . . . the lion immediately left me, and attacking Mebalwe, bit his thigh.

"Another man, whose life I had saved . . . after he had been tossed by a buffalo, attempted to spear the lion while he was biting Mebalwe . . . but at that moment the bullet he [the lion] had received took effect and he fell down dead."

STANDING GROUND

On another occasion, it was a band of armed Africans who almost took Livingstone's life. Even though he was

> ## "I was upon a little height; he [the lion] caught my shoulder as he sprang, and we both came to the ground below together."

recovering from a bout of rheumatic fever, Livingstone stood his ground and used his own gun to threaten the leader, who soon got the message. As Livingstone later wrote, "The sight of six barrels gaping into his stomach, with my own ghastly visage looking daggers into his face, seemed to produce an instant revolution in his martial feelings." Livingstone opened fire, and the party of villagers backed off. Fortunately, no one was wounded.

However well-intentioned Livingstone may have been, it is not surprising that some Africans regarded the explorer as an intruder; after all, he was on their land. Some Africans made life difficult for Livingstone, and he described them as "inveterate thieves."

Lies were told, too. On Zanzibar, one of Livingstone's porters made up a story that the missionary had died by Lake Nyasa. The false news was relayed to London. As a result, all the English newspapers featured an obituary for Livingstone, and flags were flown at half-mast in the British capital to mark his supposed passing. The rumor was disproved after Sir Roderick Murchison financed the building of a boat to search for the explorer, who was found alive and in fair health.

FAMILY TRAGEDIES

Some of the most painful episodes Livingstone experienced in Africa involved the illness and death of members of his family. In 1850, Mary gave birth to a baby girl, Elizabeth, their fourth child. The baby fell ill and died six weeks later. In his diary, Livingstone wrote, "It was the first death in our family, but just as likely to have happened had we remained at home, and we now have one of our number in heaven." To his father-in-law, he wrote, "It was like tearing out one's bowels to see her in the embrace of the King of Terrors [death]."

Illness also struck other members of the family.

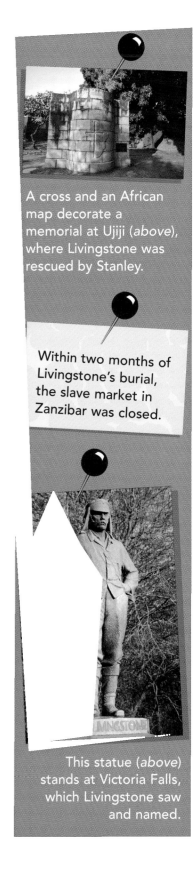

A cross and an African map decorate a memorial at Ujiji (*above*), where Livingstone was rescued by Stanley.

Within two months of Livingstone's burial, the slave market in Zanzibar was closed.

This statue (*above*) stands at Victoria Falls, which Livingstone saw and named.

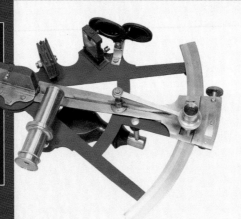

On one expedition, Livingstone got lost because of damage to his chronometers and a fault with his sextant (*right*), leading to confusion over distances and direction.

Livingstone with his wife and family at Lake Ngami (*above*). He had first arrived there a year earlier, in 1849, but decided it would be best to leave then, because the African population was unfriendly to him.

In 1872, Henry Morton Stanley went to Zanzibar to recruit men to assist Livingstone in his explorations. This engraving (*right*) shows Stanley's party gaining an audience with the Sultan.

Mary had a stroke, partly paralyzing her face. Malaria was a frequent threat. Family members got very little sleep and were always covered with mosquito bites when they woke in the morning. This was one reason why Livingstone decided to send his family back to England in 1852, not long after his wife gave birth to their son, William Oswell Livingstone.

Mary realized that she was pregnant again while she and her husband were traveling back to Africa in 1858.

The baby, Anna Mary, was born healthy at the Kuruman mission but was then sent home to Scotland to live with Livingstone's widowed mother. He did not see the child again until she was five years old. The explorer would miss his family terribly. Livingstone's own health, meanwhile, was a constant problem.

POWER POLITICS

When Livingstone began his journeys through southern Africa in the early 1840s, he was one of a small number of travelers there. As time went on, however, more and more travelers and settlers came to Africa, and the struggle for power on the continent became more intense.

Warring native cultures were always a source of concern, but Livingstone also had reason to worry about hostile slave traders. All of these were threats to British interests.

One particularly difficult time for Livingstone came in 1861, while he was unsuccessfully promoting part of southern Africa as a possible British colony. Livingstone encouraged a group of missionaries to come to the Shire

3 2115 00138 644 8

DID YOU KNOW?

Livingstone was horrified by the experience of seeing two villagers in Barotseland (present-day Zambia) seized, hacked to pieces, then thrown into a river. No crime on the villagers' part had been proven, but they were suspected of plotting against their village chief.

> *The terrible scenes of man's inhumanity to man brought on a severe headache.*

Highlands, in what is now Malawi. Not long after they arrived, the missionaries were caught in the crossfire of a native war. Then, an encounter with slave traders turned violent, and Livingstone himself had to take up arms. Later, disease claimed the life of the leader of the mission, and several other missionaries died of fever. Accused of failing to inform the newcomers of the risks they ran, Livingstone suffered a severe blow to his reputation.

Among the people most resistant to British influence in the region were the Boers, who had originally settled in South Africa as emigrant Dutch farmers. Livingstone strongly disapproved of the way the Boers seemed to regard black Africans as their personal property. He also deplored the Boers' racist attitudes, especially their view that blacks could not be educated. Not until the 1990s — more than a century later — would South African blacks free themselves from white rule and shed the burden of this racist legacy.

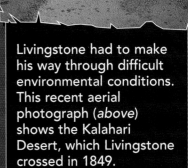

Livingstone had to make his way through difficult environmental conditions. This recent aerial photograph (*above*) shows the Kalahari Desert, which Livingstone crossed in 1849.

Henry Morton Stanley drew the original sketch from which this woodcut (*below*) of Livingstone was taken. It shows him being carried by a team of porters across a flooded river. Without their help, Livingstone would surely have drowned in the attempt.

FINDING THE FALLS

Livingstone claimed to be the first European to see Africa's superb natural wonder, Victoria Falls. This long curtain of water drops with a huge roar to the Zambezi river.

Some of Livingstone's journal notes (*above*) describe the Zambezi River and illustrate how he always kept the most meticulous records, detailing what he had seen and when.

A detail from a work by Thomas Baines (*above*) shows the bed of part of the Zambezi revealed in a dry season. Not far away, Livingstone found the mighty waterfalls he named for Queen Victoria.

Situated on the border between Zimbabwe and Zambia and so extensive that they are seen best from the air, Victoria Falls are undoubtedly Africa's main tourist attraction. Their size is awesome. Twice the size of North America's Niagara Falls, the four cataracts of

Victoria Falls are together about one mile (1.6 km) wide and drop 400 feet (242 m) into a deep gorge and into the Zambezi River.

David Livingstone first reached the Zambezi River on August 4, 1851. The Zambezi is a massive waterway, which floods

regularly and abundantly in the rainy season. Livingstone was surprised to find such a large expanse of rapidly flowing water at such a central point in Africa.

Years later, as he ventured along the upper Zambezi in a fleet of 33 canoes with Sekelutu, the Makololo chief, and 160 of Sekelutu's warriors, they passed many village settlements. Both Livingstone and Chief Sekelutu had heard of a great waterfall that lay along the Zambezi, but neither was prepared for the rainbowed cascade of falling water that greeted them.

In his journal entry for November 17, 1855, the missionary recorded stopping at one of the many islands in an archipelago within the Zambezi. There he lay down on his stomach to marvel at the scene. It was later

In prehistoric times, Africa, South America, and Antarctica were part of one huge continent that scientists call Gondwanaland. About 180 million years ago, powerful forces from within Earth caused this large land mass to break up into the southern hemisphere pattern we know today.

described by Livingstone as "the most wonderful sight I had witnessed in Africa."

To Livingstone, "The snow-white sheet [of the falling water] seemed like myriads of small comets rushing on in one direction, each of which left behind its nucleus rays of foam."

Livingstone is thought to have been the first European to see the Falls. The Africans had called them *Mosi-oa-tunya*, meaning "the smoke that thunders," a phrase that very accurately describes both their sound and

Sketched by Thomas Baines, this map (*above*) shows the route of a small boat along part of the Zambezi on the way to Tete, in what is now Mozambique. It would have required great skill to navigate past all the small islands.

This magnificent aerial photograph (*left*) is so dramatic, you can almost hear the thunderous roar of the Victoria Falls as they descend to the Zambezi River, a drop of about 400 feet (242 m).

When Livingstone saw the Kebrabasa rapids (*right*), he thought they could be navigated if the rocks they contained were blasted, but this proved impossible. Some of the rocks towered as high as 100 feet (30.5 m) above the river. His hopes of proceeding along the Zambezi were dashed, and he decided instead to explore the river's tributaries.

This painting by Thomas Baines (*above*) shows the fourth-longest river in Africa, the Zambezi. It has a total length of about 2,200 miles (3,540 km).

appearance. Livingstone gave the falls their English name to honor the British monarch, Queen Victoria. This was his way of thanking her for all the moral support she had given him.

Victoria Falls are now known to be the sixth-largest in the world by volume of water — an astonishing two million gallons per second cascade into the river below.

The multirainbow effect so often visible at Victoria Falls is due to the play of light on the crashing waters. The almost deafening sound of their cascade can be heard many miles away. Over 500,000 visitors each year view this natural wonder.

Mass tourism at the Falls, however, has been a mixed blessing. This part of Africa badly needs the income that tourism brings, but the environment, so glorious in Livingstone's day, is now under threat. Noxious fumes from traffic, radios played loudly, garbage left to litter the landscape, and detergents poured into the river all put the local environment at considerable risk today.

Victoria Falls were not the only waters given English names by Livingstone.

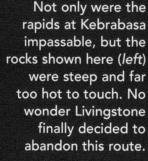

Not only were the rapids at Kebrabasa impassable, but the rocks shown here (*left*) were steep and far too hot to touch. No wonder Livingstone finally decided to abandon this route.

DID YOU KNOW?

Once he had finished marveling at Victoria Falls, David Livingstone wanted to take their measurements. Some of his instruments had broken, however, and he had forgotten how to use others. He resorted to guessing width and depth, underestimating both dimensions.

> **" It had never before been seen by European eyes; but scenes so lovely [as Africa's Victoria Falls] must have been gazed upon by angels in their flight. "**

At his suggestion, a stretch of water 33 miles (53.1 km) long became officially known as the Murchison Rapids, after Sir Roderick Murchison, another man who financially supported Livingstone.

A TRUE DISCOVERY?

Actually, no European "discovered" Victoria Falls. The Falls were already well known to the Africans who lived in the region. What we really mean when we say that a famous explorer "discovered" anything in Africa is that he or she was the first European known to have gone there.

One of Livingstone's books, *Narrative of an Expedition to the Zambezi and Its Tributaries*, undoubtedly owed much of its success

to the missionary's claim that he was the first European to explore this great river. Some historians, however, think Portuguese explorers may have been there as early as the 16th century.

Livingstone's intent, once he had found the Zambezi, was to blast away the rocks in its gorges to "open wide the gates which have barred the interior for ages." His hopes to navigate the entire river, however, were unfulfilled. Rapids at Kebrabasa, now the site of Mozambique's huge Cabora Bassa power project, made the river impassable.

A LASTING IMPACT

Victoria Falls are one of the natural wonders of the world. They are as magnificent today as they were when first sighted by Livingstone. Their roar can be heard from up to 25 miles (40 km) away. The thick mist caused by the falling water is at its most dense during the early and rainy part of the year.

Livingstone's writings on Africa, his constant efforts to end the slave trade, and his concern with the development of commerce were all to leave a lasting mark. The African countries we know today, however, did not achieve independence for a long time. From the end of the 19th century through the middle of the 20th, the map of Africa was dominated by British, French, Italian, German, Portuguese, Spanish, and Belgian colonial empires.

DETERMINED TO THE END

This sculpture, entitled *Mercy* (*above*), is one of several depicting aspects of Livingstone's life. It is on display at the Scottish National Memorial to him.

Batoka men performing a ceremonial dance (*above*). Livingstone admired many Batoka customs.

Livingstone's expeditions into Africa were expensive and dangerous, and many people wondered if they were worth it. His courage and accomplishments, however, cannot be denied.

"I will follow out the work in spite of the veto of the board. If it is according to the Will of God, means will be provided from other quarters."

When Livingstone wrote these words in a letter to a friend, he had just heard that the London Missionary Society (LMS) was to cease financing his expeditions to Africa. Such loss of support might have discouraged another man, but Livingstone, as always, refused to give up.

FORCED RESIGNATION

Withdrawal of funding by the LMS in 1857 did not come entirely as a surprise. Livingstone's quest for African converts had not been very fruitful.

Moreover, the Society had overspent the previous year and found itself in a difficult financial predicament.

Livingstone felt he had to resign his membership in the LMS, but, optimistic as always, he was sure that funds would somehow come his way. Indeed they did, with the help of an influential friend, Sir Roderick Murchison, the president of the Royal Geographical Society. Murchison, a leading scientist, was a great admirer of Livingstone's work.

Murchison took it upon himself to provide Livingstone with an introduction to the Earl of Clarendon, Britain's Foreign Secretary at the time. Lord Clarendon could not

> **It is a mistake to suppose anyone, as long as he is pious, will do as a missionary. Pioneers in everything should be the ablest and best qualified men.**

This sculpture, entitled *Courage* (*above*), depicts the challenge Livingstone would have faced when confronting people who did not know him.

have been more cooperative, and a grant was made for "exploring eastern and central Africa, for the promotion of commerce and civilization with a view to extinction of the slave trade."

PERSONAL CLASHES

Some of the personality traits that helped Livingstone survive against great odds also made him difficult to get along with. Some of the Europeans he hired for his expeditions were not very easy to get along with, either.

Taken on as a navigator for the Zambezi journey that began in 1858, Norman Bedingfeld, a high-ranking naval officer, proved to be full of self-importance and did not take kindly to orders. Livingstone described him as "a fool and a liar, and yet all

in combination with extra ostentatious piety."

When Bedingfeld was dismissed from his position, he was so up in arms that he complained about Livingstone to the Admiralty. Livingstone, however, stood his ground. A letter written by Livingstone to his former friend Bedingfeld drips with sarcasm: "With the change of climate there is often a peculiar condition of the bowels which makes the individual imagine all sorts of things in others. . . . try a little . . . medicine occasionally and you will find it much more soothing than writing official letters."

Once Bedingfeld was fired, the paddle steamer *Ma Robert* had no navigator, but Livingstone stepped into the role. He lacked experience at the helm, yet managed to navigate for the next 1,500 miles (2,414 km).

Livingstone also had a hard time getting along with the artist Thomas Baines. Matters came to a head after Baines was accused of raiding the supplies and selling them to the Portuguese. The quarrel was really quite petty, involving some missing sugar and a length of canvas.

This sculpture at the Livingstone Memorial in Scotland (*above*) shows Livingstone reading the Bible to Africans.

A sculpture of Livingstone and his family (*right*) demonstrating how to pray in the European manner.

Baines's accuser was Charles Livingstone, the missionary's brother. Almost everyone found Charles unpleasant, arrogant, and lazy. Not only was he a very difficult man, but even his brother found fault with most aspects of his work: "As an assistant he has been of no value. Photography very unsatisfactory. Magnetism still more so. Meteorological observations not creditable."

GOING TOO FAR?

As a practicing Christian, Livingstone was a man who respected Sunday as a day of rest. Normally, he would have insisted that no one work on Sunday. The pressure to get the *Ma Robert* assembled, however, was such that he put this principle aside. As usual, when faced with a strong challenge, Livingstone found a way of justifying his actions. "People, I hear, blame me for this, but they would have blamed me much more if I had lost nearly all the Expedition."

Perhaps the most stinging criticism made of David Livingstone was that voiced by John Kirk in 1862, when the explorer was trying to sail along what Kirk believed was an impassable river: "The infatuation which blinds him, I cannot comprehend . . . getting boats jammed up a river where they cannot float and where it will soon be impossible to return. It seems madness. . . . I can come to no conclusion but that Dr. L. is out of his mind."

Yet, explorers showed courage and perseverance as they explored the uncharted areas of our planet.

For Further Discussion

There are many aspects of Livingstone's travels that are thought to be controversial and therefore open to debate. The following questions can be used to guide classroom discussion.

1 Was Livingstone entitled to try to convert the peoples of Africa to Christianity, or should he have left them to their own beliefs?

2 Describe some of the dangers that Livingstone faced in Africa. How did he deal with them? Was he right in subjecting his wife and children to those same risks? What steps did he take to protect them?

3 What contribution did Livingstone make to abolition of the slave trade on the African continent?

4 How did Livingstone feel about the protection of African wildlife? Did he always live up to his principles in this matter? If not, why?

5 How successful was Livingstone as a missionary? Do you think the London Missionary Society was right to end its support for his work?

6 How did Livingstone gain the support of the British government? Why do you think the government was willing to assist him?

7 What is imperialism? Why did many of the great powers of Europe want empires in Africa?

8 To what extent did Livingstone's work help the British establish an African empire?

9 Who were Livingstone's greatest friends among the African people? Why did he like them so much, and why did they admire him?

10 What do you think were David Livingstone's greatest failings, if any?

11 What do people mean when they say that Livingstone "discovered" the Victoria Falls? Is this really accurate? Why did he give them that name?

12 What was Livingstone trying to accomplish during his last years in Africa? How well did he succeed?

13 If you had to create a new monument to the memory of Livingstone, what form would it take? Where would you place it?

14 What problems does Africa face today? All in all, do you think the period of European exploration and dominance made things better or worse for the African peoples?

MAJOR WORLD EVENTS

While Livingstone was busy exploring parts of Africa, opening trade routes, trying to put an end to the slave trade, and attempting to convert Africans to the beliefs of the Christian religion, many other events were happening in Europe, North America, and elsewhere on the globe. Find out about some of these major events (*right*), and judge how they may have affected Livingstone's accomplishments.

1841 Henry Morton Stanley was born in Wales.

1859 Charles Darwin published *On the Origin of the Species,* offering his theory of evolution.

1860 Abraham Lincoln was elected President of the United States on a platform that opposed slavery and urged the preservation of the Union.

1861 The slaveholding southern states in the United States withdrew from the Union and established the Confederacy, setting the stage for the Civil War.

1863 The Emancipation Proclamation was issued, freeing most slaves in the southern United States.

1865 The Confederacy was defeated, and Lincoln was assassinated.

The British naturalist Charles Darwin (*above*) in a cartoon making fun of his belief that humans are related to apes.

1867 The Dominion of Canada was established. Meanwhile, in Europe, Karl Marx published *Das Kapital,* a major work in the history of communism.

1877 Four years after Livingstone's death, Henry Morton Stanley reached the mouth of Africa's Congo River.

1879 Stanley returned to the Congo region, sponsored by Belgium's King Leopold II.

1904 Stanley died in London.

While Livingstone was in Africa, Abraham Lincoln (*left*) was fighting against slavery and struggling to keep the Union whole.

OVER THE YEARS

This detail (*left*) is taken from a new portrait of Livingstone based on earlier photographs of the explorer.

- Queen Victoria granted Livingstone an audience as a demonstration that Britain wholeheartedly approved of his activities in Africa.

- Livingstone was given the Freedom of the City of Edinburgh, Scotland, on September 21, 1857, in recognition of the perseverance he showed in his African journeys.

- The Royal Geographical Society awarded David Livingstone its Gold Medal to acknowledge his accomplishments.

- Livingstone's vital organs, including his heart, were buried under a tree in an African village. A carved inscription on a piece of wood taken from that tree is now held in the collection of the Royal Geographical Society.

- Livingstone was buried in Westminster Abbey, London, after his body was brought back to England. Many of Britain's greatest citizens have been entombed there, including Charles Darwin.

- Inscribed on Livingstone's tombstone are a few of the words he used during an interview given to the *New York Herald* regarding slavery. The inscription reads: "May Heaven's rich blessing come down on everyone – American, English, Turk – who will help heal this open Sore of the World."

- The award-winning David Livingstone Centre is situated at his birthplace in Blantyre, near Glasgow, Scotland. Housed in an 18th-century building, exhibits cover events from his earliest years and include the one-room apartment that served as his childhood home.

- Exhibits at the Livingstone Centre also portray his discoveries and missionary work in Africa. Some of his navigational instruments and medical equipment can be seen there, too.

"You have accomplished more for the happiness of mankind than has been done by all the African travelers hitherto put together." This was the eulogy received by David Livingstone from his friend, Astronomer Royal Thomas Maclear. During his lifetime and after his death, Livingstone received many great honors (*left*).

GLOSSARY

archipelago: a group of islands or an area of sea containing many islands.

astronomer: someone who studies the stars, planets, and other aspects of space.

baptized: having received the ritual that admits a person into the Christian community.

botanist: a specialist in the understanding of plant life.

caravan: a group of travelers on a journey.

cataracts: waterfalls.

chronometer: an instrument for measuring time with great accuracy.

civilized: having a high level of technological development and culture.

colony: a settlement of people away from their parent government.

commerce: the buying and selling of goods on a large scale.

converts: people who have changed from one religion to another.

countenances: faces.

dhow: a type of Arab ship.

dysentery: an infection of the intestines that causes severe diarrhea.

economic: relating to the production, distribution, and consumption of goods and services.

emigrant: a person who leaves one country to live in another.

eminent: known as being well thought of or superior.

enlightened: freed of ignorance and fully understanding all problems involved.

eternal optimist: always thinking the best will come of any situation.

etiquette: the procedure for doing things in a proper or acceptable way.

evangelist: a minister.

expedition: a journey taken for a specific purpose.

exploited: made use of something or someone for one's own advantage and at the expense of someone else.

extinction: the condition of no longer existing.

ferment: to undergo or cause a chemical breakdown that changes something to alcohol.

Gondwanaland: in prehistoric times, a huge land mass in the southern hemisphere.

gorge: a steep canyon.

hemisphere: half of the globe divided through the center, either at the equator (to make northern and southern hemispheres) or at a meridian (to make eastern and western hemispheres).

humanitarian: a person who shows traits of kindness and promotes human welfare.

inveterate: firmly established as or habitual.

ivory: the valuable substance of an elephant's tusks.

Koran: the holy book of the Muslims, also spelled Qur'an.

legacy: something received from an earlier generation.

malaria: a disease of chills and fever transmitted to humans by a particular type of mosquito.

meticulous: paying careful attention to detail.

mission: where a missionary operates.

missionaries: people who set out to convert others to their own religion.

Muslim: a follower of the religion of Islam.

obituary: a newspaper notice about someone's death that often describes the achievements of that person.

obsessive: worrying unreasonably about something.

ostentatious piety: a display of religious beliefs in a showy way.

palliative: something that eases pain or relieves the symptoms of a disease.

plundered: taken away from or stolen by force.

porters: people who are employed to carry things.

poverty: the state of being poor or not having enough money.

rapids: swift-flowing parts of a river where the current runs over rocks.

rheumatic fever: a disease, usually occurring among children, that can cause permanent heart damage.

scrubland: an area or landscape where vegetation consists mostly of small trees and shrubs.

sextant: a scientific instrument for measuring angular distances and generally used by navigators for determining their position.

sultan: a ruler, usually of a Muslim state.

tenement: usually located in a city, an apartment building that offers few comforts.

tributaries: streams that feed larger streams or lakes.

visage: the face.

yoke: a wooden frame around the heads and necks of individuals (usually cattle).

FOR FURTHER STUDY

BOOKS

David Livingstone. C. S. Nicholls (Sutton)

King Leopold's Ghost: A Story of Greed, Terror, and Heroism in Colonial Africa. Adam Hochschild (Houghton Mifflin)

The Scramble for Africa: White Man's Conquest of the Dark Continent from 1876 to 1912. Thomas Pakenham (Random House)

Stanley and Livingstone and the Exploration of Africa in World History. Richard Worth (Enslow Publishers)

VIDEOS AND DVDS

Biography: Stanley and Livingstone. (A&E Entertainment)

Great Adventurers: David Livingstone — Journey to the Heart of Africa. (Kultur Films)

National Geographic: Africa. (Warner Home Video)

The New Explorers: In the Footsteps of Dr. Livingstone. (A&E Home Video)

WEB SITES

David Livingstone School Multimedia Project. atschool.eduweb.co.uk/blantyre/living/livmenu.html

Dr. David Livingstone: Missionary, Explorer, Social Crusader. www.innercite.com/~rlivingston/dr_dave.htm

The Great Zambezi River www.africa-insites.com/zambia/travel/Places/ZambeziR.htm

National Geographic Presents Forbidden Territory. www.nationalgeographic.com/lantern/